nature's friends

Ants

by Ann Heinrichs

Content Adviser: Janann Jenner, Ph.D.

Science Adviser: Terrence E. Young Jr., M.Ed., M.L.S., Jefferson Parish (La.) Public Schools

Reading Adviser: Dr. Linda D. Labbo, Department of Reading Education, College of Education, The University of Georgia

COMPASS POINT BOOKS

MINNEAPOLIS, MINNESOTA

Compass Point Books
3722 West 50th Street, #115
Minneapolis, MN 55410

Visit Compass Point Books on the Internet at *www.compasspointbooks.com*
or e-mail your request to *custserv@compasspointbooks.com*

Photographs ©: Dwight Kuhn, cover, 1, 12–13, 18–19; Bill Beatty, 4–5, 6–7; S. Strickland/
Visuals Unlimited, 8; Mark Moffett/Minden Pictures, 10–11, 22–23; Gallo Images/Corbis,
14–15; Richard Thom/Visuals Unlimited, 16–17; Australian Picture Library/Corbis, 20–21;
J. Serrao/Visuals Unlimited, 24–25; Robert & Linda Mitchell, 26–27.

Editors: E. Russell Primm and Emily J. Dolbear
Photo Researchers: Svetlana Zhurkina and Jo Miller
Photo Selector: Linda S. Koutris
Designer: The Design Lab

Library of Congress Cataloging-in-Publication Data

Heinrichs, Ann.
 Ants / by Ann Heinrichs.
  p. cm. — (Nature's friends)
 Includes bibliographical references (p.   ).
 Summary: Introduces distinguishing characteristics, life cycles, and different types of ants.
 ISBN 0-7565-0164-4 (hardcover)
 1. Ants—Juvenile literature. [1. Ants.] I. Title. II. Series: Heinrichs, Ann. Nature's friends.
QL568.F7 H45 2002
595.79'6—dc21   2001004971

© 2002 by Compass Point Books

Printed in the United States of America.

Table of Contents

Amazing Ants

Here come the ants! See how they march in long lines. You see them in the garden and in the woods. You may even see them in your house.

Ants have lived on Earth for more than 100 million years. Today, ants live almost everywhere in the world. But you won't find ants living where it's very, very cold.

Ants are amazing because they work together so well. Each ant has at least one job. They all work to help one another live.

◂ *Black ants work together.*

How Ants Are Built

An ant's body is hard on the outside. The hard part is the **exoskeleton.** It protects the ant's body. Ants have three main body parts—the head, the **thorax,** and the abdomen.

An ant's head has two big **compound eyes** and a mouth. Its antennae, or feelers, are on top of its head.

The thorax is the middle part of the ant. Three pairs of legs grow there. Some kinds of ants have wings on the thorax, too.

The abdomen is the large back section. This is where the ant's stomach is.

The ant's body has three main parts. ▶

How Ants Talk, Smell, and Hear

Ants cannot speak, but they can give one another messages. They do it by touching their feelers together.

Ants know who their friends are by smelling them. Ants find food by smell too. But they do not have noses. They smell with their feelers! Some kinds of ants are blind. They find their way around by smelling.

Ants have no ears either. They hear by feeling **vibrations.** Their feelers and other body parts feel vibrations.

◄ Ants can communicate by touching their feelers together.

Ants at Home

Ants live in groups called colonies. Most ant colonies live under the ground. That's where they build their nests.

An ant's nest has many tunnels. The tunnels are like roads. They lead to underground rooms. Some rooms are used to store food. Other rooms are used to raise young ants.

An ant nest with tunnels and chambers ▶

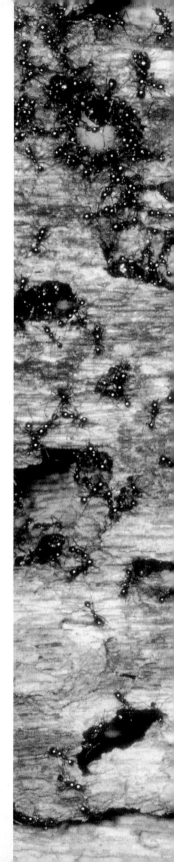

Ants at Work

Every ant in the colony has a job. The most important ant is the queen ant. She lays eggs. A **larva** hatches out of each egg. It changes to a **pupa** and then to an adult ant.

Most of the ants in a colony are worker ants. They are all females. They take care of the queen and find food. They also build and repair the colony's walls. Soldiers are extra-large workers. They protect the colony from enemies.

Male ants do not work. They **mate** with the queen so that she can lay eggs. Then they die.

◄ *An ant takes care of the pupae that will soon become adult ants.*

Army Ants

Army ants are scary! Thousands of army ants march together across the ground. They eat every insect in their path. They may even eat the remains of mice, birds, or bigger animals.

Army ants do not build nests. They keep moving most of the time. Sometimes they stop so that the queen can lay eggs. When the eggs hatch, the army ants march on again.

Ants eat a small mammal. ▶

Leaf-Cutter Ants

Leaf-cutter ants are farmers. They plant gardens in their underground nests. There they grow **fungi.** Fungi are molds and mushrooms. The ants eat the fungi.

To make a garden, worker ants find pieces of leaves. They carry them into the nest and chew them into a paste. They place some fungi on the chewed-up leaves. Soon the fungi grow into a garden.

◀ *A tropical leaf-cutter ant carries a piece of a leaf back to the nest.*

Dairying Ants

Some ants are like farmers who raise cows for milk. These ants are called dairying ants. They are named after dairies, where cows are milked.

Dairying ants keep tiny insects called aphids. The aphids give off a sweet liquid called **honeydew.** Some people say this process is like cows giving milk.

When an ant wants honeydew, it gently rubs an aphid with its feelers. Then the honeydew comes out of the aphid. The ant sucks up the honeydew. It stores the liquid inside its body. Then it feeds honeydew to other ants.

An ant rubs aphids with its feelers to release honeydew. ▶

Honey Ants

A honey ant sucks honeydew from plants or licks it from insects. Then the ant goes back to its nest. There it finds a special honey ant worker called a replete. The ant pumps honeydew from its mouth into the replete's mouth.

The replete is like a big bottle. It stores honeydew in its body for other ants to eat. A replete swells up so much that it cannot move.

◀ *A replete honey ant swollen with honeydew.*

Ants that Keep Slaves

Some ants are called slave makers. They make other ants work for them.

Slave-maker ants march to another nest and start a fight. They fight until they can steal young ant pupae from the other nest. Then they carry the young ones back with them.

When the stolen ants grow up, they work in their new home. They find food for their masters.

Slave-maker ants carry stolen young back to the nest. ▶

Carpenter Ants

A human carpenter builds things out of wood. But carpenter ants do not build. They chew tunnels through wood to make their nests.

Carpenter ants make nests in rotten tree stumps or logs. Some make their nests in living trees. This kills the tree. Carpenter ants may even chew tunnels into the wooden parts of a house.

◀ *Carpenter ants tunnel through a piece of wood.*

Ants Can Be Our Friends

Some ants are scary. Others make big problems for humans. But ants can be helpful, too. Ants eat insects that kill farmers' crops. Ants' nests break up the soil so air and water can get in.

Scientists study ants because their way of life is so interesting. You can study them, too. You can watch them outdoors. Or you can buy an ant farm in a pet store. Have fun!

A new colony built by leaf-cutter ants in Texas ▶

Glossary

compound eyes—eyes that are made up of many tiny eyes

exoskeleton—the hard covering on the outside of an animal's body that gives support and protection

fungi—organisms that live on dead plants and animals

honeydew—a sugary substance left on plant leaves by certain insects or fungi

larva—the wormlike form an insect takes after hatching from an egg and before becoming a pupa

mate—to join together to produce young

pupa—the form an insect takes after being a larva and before becoming an adult

thorax—the middle part of an insect's body

vibrations—very fast back-and-forth movements

Let's Look at Ants

Class: Insecta
Order: Hymenoptera
Family: Formicidae
Species: about 20,000 known species

Range: Ants are found in almost all parts of the world. They are most abundant in tropical zones.

Life span: Average life span is less than six months though some worker and queen ants may live for several years.

Life stages: Eggs are laid by queen ants. Life stages are egg, larva, pupa, and adult.

Food: Most ants are omnivorous—they eat plants as well as animals.

At risk: Forty-five species of ants are currently considered at risk because of habitat destruction.

Did You Know?

Queen ants are born with wings. They break off after mating.

So many ants live in the Amazon rain forests that their total weight is about four times more than the combined weight of all of the birds, reptiles, mammals, and amphibians in the area.

In 1998, the oldest-known ant fossil was found in New Jersey. It is about 92 million years old.

Myrmecology is the name given to the scientific study of ants.

The heart of an ant is a long tube. It pumps the blood from the rear of the ant to the head.

An ant's blood is colorless.

The ants in the animated film *A Bug's Life* have only four legs. Real ants have six legs.

Junior Entomologists

Entomologists are scientists who study insects. You can be an entomologist, too! Try this simple experiment. You will need a notebook, a pen or pencil, and a magnifying glass. You will also need $\frac{1}{2}$ teaspoon of sugar, $\frac{1}{2}$ teaspoon of honey, and a $\frac{1}{2}$ teaspoon of chocolate syrup. Go outside and find an anthill. Place the sugar, the honey, and the chocolate syrup on the ground near the anthill. Watch the ants to see if they like one of these foods more than the others. Use the magnifying glass to get a closer look at the ants during your experiment.

Now try to answer these questions:

Was one of the three foods you put out their favorite?

   Which one?

How did you decide this was their favorite?

What other foods would you like to experiment with?

What color were the ants you were observing?

How big were they?

How many body parts did they have?

How many legs did they have?

Do you think other kinds of ants would have the same favorite food?

   Why or why not?

Draw a picture of an ant.

Want to Know More?

AT THE LIBRARY

Coughlan, Cheryl. *Ants.* Mankato, Minn.: Pebble Books, 1999.

Demuth, Patricia Brennan, and S. D. Schindler (illustrator). *Those Amazing Ants.*
New York: Simon & Schuster, 1994.

Fowler, Allan. *Inside an Ant Colony.* Danbury, Conn.: Children's Press, 1998.

ON THE WEB

AntCam

http://www.antcam.com/

To see a carpenter ant colony at work and learn more about ants

Ant Colonies

http://www.antcolony.org/

Tells all about life in an ant colony and about different kinds of ants

Gakken's Photo Encyclopedia: Ants

http://ant.edb.miyakyo-u.ac.jp/INTRODUCTION/Gakken79E/Page_02.html

For great pictures and information about ants

THROUGH THE MAIL

Center for Insect Science Education Outreach

University of Arizona

Life Sciences South 225

P.O. Box 210106

Tucson, AZ 85721-0106

520/621-9310

ON THE ROAD

The Philadelphia Insectarium

8046 Frankford Avenue

Philadelphia, PA 19136

215/338-3000

To view ants among the
many other insect exhibits
at this all-bug museum

Smithsonian Institution

O. Orkin Insect Zoo

National Museum of
Natural History

Constitution Avenue and
10th Street, N.W.

Washington, DC 20560

202/357-2700

To view insect exhibits that
include a leaf-cutter ant colony

Index

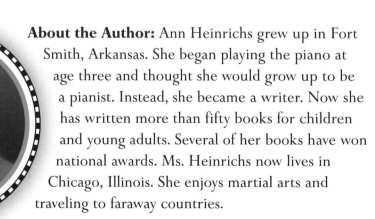

About the Author: Ann Heinrichs grew up in Fort Smith, Arkansas. She began playing the piano at age three and thought she would grow up to be a pianist. Instead, she became a writer. Now she has written more than fifty books for children and young adults. Several of her books have won national awards. Ms. Heinrichs now lives in Chicago, Illinois. She enjoys martial arts and traveling to faraway countries.